Supreme

Lynnette Elizabeth Johnson

Supreme
Written by Lynnette Elizabeth Johnson
April 2017
Cover photo by Keith Claytor timefrozen.com

This book is dedicated to the women; all of us.

SUPREME
Table of Contents

Supreme

Do you remember the exact moment you
realized your power?
How bout when that lil' baby stopped hollerin
soon as it laid its pretty eyes on you?
The first time your presence lifted the air in the
room?
Your voice cracked the silence
You made something happen with a thought
You made somebody's day by giving them the
time of day
You don't even wear a watch
They was grinning
You did that
Remember that time
the entire planet paused when you showed up
in that dress?
It was an old dress too
You tossed your hair over your shoulder and
the clouds rolled back so the sun could catch a
glimpse of your neck and kiss on it
The ocean eased up to let you in, wanted you to
stay the night
You let the stars count your beauty marks -
eleven
The wind caught your fragrance and pushed it
out into the trees
Birds started singing, fighting over solos

Tried to lull you to sleep
They didn't know you could sing too
Them birdies got quiet and took notes
You are a wonder
Woman
Remember that

Sometimes

Sometimes when I'm walking
I swing my hips
extra
for no particular reason
except
to collect the electricity
my thighs
create when they slide around each other
remind myself
of my power
even my jeans get weak at the seams
when I move too much
It's like can't no thing or nobody handle all of
this
I am magic
I might could
accidentally set the whole world on fire
If I don't be still
Sometimes, you can't tell me nothing
even a compliment would fall on deaf ears
because I already know
an insult would tickle me
because
lies always make me laugh
I know displaying magic
can be a trigger
for folk who ain't got their own
too bad I don't care.

Disclaimer

Get from round here with that temporary
enthusiasm
I don't want none of your "let's try and see
where this can go."
Keep your tenderness to yourself if it is only an
introductory offer
My affection does not come in trial size
You cannot return it if it don't fit the way you
thought it would
Don't kiss me like that again
less you plan on making anniversaries with me
there is no mention of forever in your whispers
you not about to pull me in
then shake me loose
when this graduates from recreation
to responsibility
that's how folk end up hurt
oh
not me
I'm thinking of you
and your tires
and your position at your job
and
any other woman you think you might want to
call companion in the imaginary future you
ain't ready to discuss yet
all of that is in danger of getting cut up
if you are just pretending

If you the type to dangle authenticity and
connection in my face and snatch it back
watch yourself
I am not built for short-term romance
love is not supposed to expire
call it what it is
and take it somewhere else
If I am not The One
I'm not the one.

Too Much

There is just way too much flava
in the food
in the hair
in the mourning and in the joy
our noise is too distinct our language is so extra
we are the most
even when we are few our voices volume
majority
our faces are imprinted in memories
you gon see us in a room
our bodies our lips our skin our blood-
everybody wants it
we stand like there are titanium rods in our
backs
we recover like pain is not a deterrent
we celebrate like this may be the last party
we are too much
all this flavor in our stories
in our love
in our praise
God wanted spice and testimony and colorful
worship
and
He wanted to see Himself
so He made us
we just like Him

Nerves
"I am tolerating you right now"
No one ever says that
Patience is inside work
Clenched molars
Tight abdominal muscles
Empathetic understanding
Eyes NOT rolling all the way to the back of your
head
Cuss words pinched and pushed back into
throat
Deliberate breathing
You ever been in the middle of this selfless act
of love and have said irritant express their
frustration towards you?
You?
Are tiring of ME?
Here you are
righteous
hoping for recognition of your restraint
an applause for your endurance
a reward for your poise
and all this time you were clawing chalk boards
and popping gum on another
and they have run out of nerves
ain't that some shit?

A Tale of Two Titties

boobies
breasticles
tits
knockers
The Girls
The Talent
mine
his
milk machines
magic
they refused to succumb to puberty
flat and defiant they rested against rib cage
their nonexistence
hidden best as could be
puffy tops
frilly sweaters
swimsuits were unforgiving
they did not care about insecurities
or a 13 year old girl's prayers
or middle school
or HIGH school
or boys
or the locker room
thought they would never show
but they popped up
pert and full of life
one B cup
one A and a half

just in time for prom
they been pushed
groped
stuffed
poked
cut
tested
restrained
high and lifted up
decorated
decoration
engorged
deflated
nourishment
party starters
and tranquilizers
they are amazing
They could tell a few stories
But they won't

So High

I don't smoke weed but
Kissing
a killer poem
my son snoring in my bed
my man taking me away for a little bit
the sun on my face early and sticking around
waiting for me to get off work so we could vibe
some more
Detroit Deli turned up windows rolled down
My girls calling to tell me they in love
Discovering new kindred spirits
Talenti vanilla caramel swirl straight out the
container
An unexpected check in the mail
New lipstick
Laughing till I can't breathe
Finding something I was missing
Finding out nothing is missing
Counting my blessings
- will have me feeling easy

Elliott

Ours is a love that was decided
an arrangement
I would wait
he would arrive
we each played our parts to perfection
we did not need instruction on how to
communicate
I learned his language
I taught him mine
He is demanding, clumsy and fearless
I am not
but we match
every day is surprise and reward
a discovery on his part
whenever his mind catches hold of a thing
for the first time
I see it again as brand new
bugs and stone are relevant
he is a gift
his questions increasingly more complicated
I love him today
separate from his time under my heart
stretching my abdomen kicking my insides
separate from our blood connection that will
always be
I love who he is right now
his palate
his opinions

he is mine
but
he does not belong to me
he is his own self
I am my own self
we are solid

So, you think you can poem?
You are proficient in cadence and verse
You are clever in metaphor
But all you seem to have in your pen is ink
There is no lightning in your keystrokes
Your journal is not a weapon of mass
destruction
What you did was cute
-but
That was not a poem
It was too measured
There was no blood
No trigger
No baptism
How do you expect to save yourself with such
congeniality?
Where is the desperation?
Poem is suture for severed artery
Poem is prostrate at the altar
Not applause and spotlight
Poem is cardiac arrest and resuscitation
It is urgent and vile, lovely and wild, anarchy
and disrespectful
It is charge and conviction
You didn't even die a little
Nobody did
Come back with some suffering
Some secret and shame
Bring a blowtorch

And a couple of muthafuckas
You can still wear those pink stilettos
Tuck a flower behind your ear if you must
But get all the way naked
Swirl some ugly with that cute
Show no mercy
It is better if this scares you
You cannot be brave if you are fearless
Besides
Sweat and piss is good seasoning for poem
Put some samurai in your stanzas
Lay some Shaka Zulu battle cries on that
iambic pentameter
Banish a demon with your confession
Make Harriet Tubman wanna raise up from the
dead just to buy a t-shirt with your image on it
Choke a molester with your wordplay
Skin a racist zombie alive with your
switchblade tongue
Save sugar and spice for cupcakes
Woman
You want to call yourself a poet?
You'll have to bleed somebody in this bitch
And that somebody
Is supposed to be you.

Control

I may have inadvertently fit a little too much
pride in my survival kit
That's the only reason I drank my drink
I thought the Goose and cranberry would have
been far more delicious
stinging your eyes
and dripping down your neck
maybe you would have slipped on an ice cube
in a futile attempt to escape my wordless
cocktail toss
in
your
face
The idea alone had me good and drunk
I measured the stride it would take to reach you
4 paces
3 seconds
A swift and memorable assault on your persona
in public
could backfire...
People would know for certain I was feeling
And may misinterpret my dramatic display
as the tantrum of a jilted lover
nah
I need my rage to be recognized and respected
My fury is not born of broken heart and
unrequited desire
I stays requited

My indignation is righteous
I wouldn't want anyone to think I wanted you
anymore
I wouldn't want you to think I wanted you
anymore
So I drank my drink
And the only burning in your eyes that night
was the view of your tired looking date
soo tired
kinda like your excuses
Y'all match
i'm so glad you found each other
Maybe she can help you find my money

Block

I don't want to write another poem about a
man
They get all the poetry
too bad
my pen won't even work right
if I don't drag his name across a page first
I don't want him to get credit for being the root
of my pain
He don't deserve the shine
He may get confused and list it as an
accomplishment
put it on a resume
ask for royalties
He ain't my joy either
I have lots of good reasons to smile that have
nothing to do with something sweet he said
people say sweet shit all the time
he ain't the only one
this poem is not about him
It's not about anything
I have nothing to write about today

Pre-Grown

Only because we were all mostly just children
when you think of it that way
you can almost pardon our ignorance
it is scary when someone is doing a thing we
have been told we ain't supposed to do
When someone is just being their own self
their own natural self
minding their own business
and living their own life in the way that they
would want to do it
and it collides with everything that you was
growed up with in the little home town where
you from
it don't fit the religion and woman-ness and
man-ness and shame and right and not right
and all that you know to be true in the world
and this is coming after you had been deemed
one of the best and the brightest
and just before you discovered you were
exceedingly average and really don't know too
much of anything
and you encounter a Redley
sauntering across campus
absorbing all of the hope and possibility and
the historical blackness up out the cobblestone
just like you
exploring their talent and brilliance like you
getting great

like you
but sauntering unapologetically flipping long
extensions over shoulder
waving and laughing with a lightness that was
woman
and a voice that was man
another grown child misidentified his own
confusion and embarrassment for anger and
disgust
he was caught licking his lips and prepping his
introduction
drawn in by the beckoning and hypnotic sashay
of Redley
when he thought he knew who he was looking
at from behind
maybe if there had not been a small audience
he may have been able to explore this new
concept in a gentle way
the way his mother would want him to behave
but he was not quite grown up enough to be the
kind of man he could be proud of
so he said something mean
and I may have laughed but I was a child too
I loved Redley later
I wonder if he remembers me laughing at him
before I was laughing with him and cheering
for him and praying for him
He describes college days as "not ALL bad"

I hate the part I may have played in any day
that was struggle for him
we learned so much in college
I wish everyone could have had a chance to go
and grow up.

Give up the Ghost

She counted backwards from nine staring at a tropical sunset torn from a calendar so thoughtfully taped to the ceiling. It was peeling away in one corner. She wondered how long it had been there. It may fall soon. The idea of a tired, tattered, faded, sunset refusing to participate and giving up the ghost, in the middle of her time here was so tragically hilarious she laughed herself to sleep. Grateful for the distraction, she didn't travel to a beach in her dream but she was able to find something funny. That was a sign. She woke up in triage. A room of wounded women crying and moaning and coming to, she was relieved. It was finished. He was waiting outside. She had forgotten about him until she saw his face. She was tempted to laugh again at herself, at the carelessness, at the picketers carrying Jackson Pollock paintings and chanting, calling her names. Telling her to get back in her car, return to wherever she came from and start a family like the good Lord wanted her to. They wasn't passing out jobs, or solutions, or comfort, or money or partners or support. Just judgment. And those paintings were not actually paintings up close. She was Pro Life too. She chose her life that day. She didn't regret it then. She don't regret it now.

FIN

Aunt's peach cobbler, everybody's favorite,
don't taste right Big Tony's stories wasn't funny
today, couldn't even muster up a fake chuckle
the sun is too bright, noisy-bright

best outfit, looks tacky, cheap, don't fit right
whole earth off kilter Wednesday and Thursday
came and went sleep didn't

he could make it all better he knows he could
the timbre of his voice is a lullaby and a
morning song the way he hums when he eats
makes you want to cook him something
delicious while you wearing something pretty
and smelling sweet

his stereotypical man-ness; rough hands, foul
mouth, quick temper, hairy everything

brought out a different side in you, a quiet
calm, a few extra pounds
he left a storm in his wake

you wished you could take back all the
vulnerability you laid out on the counter
wished you could retract every statement of
answered prayer and best you ever so he

couldn't walk around knowing you will never
get anyone to love you good as he tried to do it

you wish somebody had taught you how to
keep somebody's heart in your hand
how to de-escalate an argument
how to believe somebody when they are telling
you the hand-to-God truth
how to not want somebody who don't want you
no more
how to be fine with all this extra room in the
bed and the closet
how to behave like everything is normal when
nothing is how it should be

all of a sudden chewing is complicated, getting
up out the bed is too much to ask, crying and
breathing are pretty much the same thing

he had convinced you, you were worthy of love
and then
he changed his mind

Three Ring

I used to think
Couldn't nobody ignore an elephant in a room
the way I could do it
But together
We a circus act
cramming so many beautiful beasts into this
tiny space
acting like it ain't funky in here
struggling to breathe through painted smiles
juggling shit
they are a drunken horn section startling us out
of our pretend sleep
serenading us
they dance on our feet
we are clumsy and choreographed
moving out of their way
this is an unnecessary crazy
we know that
but
this is all we know

Derailed

Derailed Distressed Distracted
Off Track
Off the beaten path
Off
On off on
Off again
Disappointment demoted Diminished
Dumb Drunk Damaged
Devalued Detached
Dead inside
Dafuq
Deez Nutz
You are closer than you were when you started
Determined
Your path is winding road
Hurdle and canyon
Risk and riddle
And right and wrong turn
And even your wrong turns were divine
intervention
You right here
You are delivered
You s'posed to be exactly where you is
It is not too late
For you
You gone be alright
Your prayers are still righteous
Devout

You are no less deserving
You are no less
Your death day is a million miles away on foot
You not even as old as you thought you was
And ooh the stories you will tell them when you
get where you going
Getting derailed was a gift
It was the best thing that could have happened
It was the only thing that could have happened
What in the world are you crying about?

Through his Stomach
Three
Whole
Cakes
turned upside-down in the trash
one after the other

First one dry
2nd one moist and nasty
Third one burnt on the top and cracked down
the middle
Fourth one was perfection
Carrot cake

She overheard him telling somebody his
grandmama used to make a wonderful cake
took the recipe with her when she went home
to Glory
Thanksgiving ain't been the same in six years
She set it in the lounge
Took her break same time as his
They all sat around smackin they lips slurping
coffee and complimenting her
-cept for him
"Have some cake man. I made it." she offered,
as casually as she was able
Snatched her daydreams right out the air when
he declined
Not a big fan of carrot he claimed

"Looks right though" he tried to recover, when he saw the light move off her face. "Reminds me of my grandma." he slid out the room
She didn't know what to do with herself
Went back to her desk
Found another recipe
See if he like chocolate
Dusted off her daydream
she had six months to get an invitation to holiday dinner
He gon eat some of her cake
He gon love it

Experiment
He is a scientist
only explanation
for his continuous testing of the sturdiness of
my love
he must believe it indestructible
he stretches it translucent
starves it
drops it from the rooftops of skyscrapers
over and
over
it doesn't shatter
I want to read the results of his findings
how much neglect
the exact amount of broken promise
totality of withheld affection
he predicts it would take to destroy it
if he had asked
I could have told him
saved him some time and energy
research
resilient hearts run in my family
all the women got em
you can't break it
it will never decrease in size or power
But
it can certainly move

OK

Because she was starving
And he was hearty, and warm and available
She spoke "just this once, ok?"
Intending to sound authoritative and confirm
there was comprehension - with "ok "
She wanted him to know this was a first for her
and she loved LOVED her man
However
He wasn't able to sate her hunger or quiet the
lonely - that's what she meant by "ok"
But it came out sounding more like a request
for permission
He could grant it but
He had been waiting a very long time for her
Her man must ain't know what to do with that
"Just this once" pushed passed her teeth all
breathy
He smiled with half his mouth
He should leave, right now
His fingers paused on the place on her back
where every nerve ended and began
Loosely
so she could feel free
but she felt pinned
critical thought absent
the window closed
she wasn't prepared hadn't groomed herself the
way she would have done if she had known

her hair was wild about her head
she was too hungry to feel shame
"breathe" he said
she cried
and he let her
and she slept
and he held her
and she woke
and he was still there
and she was full

APB

I would like to report myself missing
ain't seen hide nor hare of me
since...
I don't know when
Been known to disappear on occasion
just watch my phone ring until it stops
skip makeup
eat junk
fold up my genuine smile and stuff it between
the mattresses
carry the bootleg one
all teeth
no eyes
mechanical laugh
but I always come back
but this time
I may have slipped into some type of vortex
I thought maybe I was just down because
Prince died
but that shouldn't have taken me out like that
I cried too much about it
I counted my blessings
but, gratitude and guilt are strange companions
what I look like all forlorn with all this
goodness around me?
all teeth
no eyes
somebody better find me.

Exceptional

Transcends race
I know that magic
A crown reserved for having an undeniable
talent for making people see beyond your
blackness straight to your humanity
You are practically levitating
When you are in the room and they are not
uncomfortable
The intention is compliment
The Something about you
For me it has always been
The way my speaking words are not elongated
or cut and reworked
The way I never seem angry
The surprise that is not always masked
when the person on the other end of the phone
has the opportunity to greet me in person
when they find out my zip code
or my mother's connections
when they like me
when I like them
when they discover how much we have in
common
when I reveal how much we don't
the paradigm shift
when they catch themselves
"you're nothing like..."
- pause

nappy as my hair is?
ebony as my flesh is?
rhythmic as my walk is?
resilient as I am?
way my fingers stayed curled tight for days
when they broke that boys back in Baltimore?
way I turned that fifteen cents into forty-five
thousand dollars?
I am as black as you want to pretend I am not
I am as black as your fears
Black as the man you hope your daughter never
brings home
Black as the bad news at 11
Black as Katrina
Black as Jesus
Black as Michelle Obama and Serena and
Venus
and Prince
Black as chattel slavery
Black as the picture of poverty that hangs in the
back of your mind
and still as human as you
still as bleed if you cut me
still as in love with my children
still as dreaming of a brighter future
as you
It's not a compliment

Word

We do not all have full juicy lips
or skin as deep and dark as the soil
all our hair don't transform in water or grow
upwards
all our women ain't shaped like guitars
all our men aren't endowed like wild horses
we did not all spend summers south of the
Mason-Dixon
or learn how to fight in Brooklyn
we cannot all jump double-dutch
we did not all matriculate at an HBCU
or cut our teeth on Dubois and Baldwin or
hooks
some of our backsides are unfamiliar with the
sting of leather
we have not all had our heads popped with
wide tooth combs while sitting between the
shiny knees of a mother who just wants the
parts straight and we wigglin
or bout sprain our own necks making the
colorful beads on our braids click and clack
click-clack
we can't all run fast
all of us don't know what to do with a
basketball
We can't all dance on beat
we don't all like colla-greens
we don't all have play cousins

42

all our daddies ain't dead or doing bids
we ain't all baptized in the name of The Father,
The Son and the Holy Spirit
we do not all identify the other brown face in a
sea of beige as ally
we ain't all voting for the same candidate
we ain't all voting
we ain't all broke
we ain't all mad at R Kelly
might think Sandra Bland shoulda just been
more cooperative
think Obama is to blame for everything wrong
with the country
I know this
we are not all the same
we do not all speak the same language
there is not a singular way to be Black in
America
we don't even all call ourselves Black
you can think Prince is overrated
vote for Donald Trump
or believe nobody has worn cornrows better
than a Kardashian
you can eat just anybody's potato salad
you don't have to jump the broom or do the
electric slide at your wedding
and still be able to trace your lineage to Marcus
Garvey
that's your inalienable right

your business
but
what brand of Negro
allows their white friends to toss around the
word nigger
like a baseball in the park?
where are You from?
Who made you?
It don't turn your stomach?
Why don't it repulse you?
You don't feel itchy or ashamed when they say
it and smile?
Does it not sound like the moans echoing from
the belly of the Good Ship Jesus?
Doesn't sound like children being yanked from
crying mother's arms to you?
That word doesn't feel like broken neck uncles
dangling from trees to you?
Doesn't sound like jingling chains on auction
blocks and missing humanity?
Doesn't sound like night riders and hooded
horsemen when they say it?
Doesn't sting like hot spit on a face at a
Woolworth counter?
Doesn't rhyme with oppression to you?
When white folk say it, it can't mean comrade
Can't mean sister
Can't mean "I know your struggle"
Can't mean "we share a burden"

It can only mean one thing
It means you are a fool
or somebody failed you
It don't swing from slur to hip-hip hop when
they say it
Dropping the R ain't the same as dropping a
flux capacitor in a DeLorean
you can't travel time and change history and
give it new meaning
I know why they want to
it's because some of us
make everything look delicious
making smoking look cool as fuck
make prison and poverty seem a little bit sexy
make
pig innards into a delicacy
they want to be down with the dexterity
inner circle-secret handshake-know all the
words to every Public Enemy song-I named my
son Cassius —down
But it don't work like that
matter of fact it is reminder of the divide
there is no context that loosens the roots
it is treason
to allow this
this is not Black
you are not Black

You are something else.

Evidence

It is my prayer that it is never my turn
But if they should come for me
If I should roll through a stop sign
Or offend a white woman
Or ask a stranger for help in the middle of the
night
Or be at prayer meeting
Or swimming
Or selling something I ain't sposed to be selling
If they should decide my lungs are taking up
too much good air
If my earthly presence makes them feel too
much like alien
If suggesting there is too much abuse of their
assigned, not
inherent authority, is received as disrespect
and threat
Before everything goes dark
I hope my fear summons the spirit of my
wildest ancestor
May she inhabit my body in the final hours
Make sure it ain't an easy victory
Make sure they know this is not gonna be no
small thing
Make sure they know at the end of me there is
the beginning of
nightmare

We will curse them with vivid and recurring
dreams that become premonition
burning buildings
And folk turning up missing
You all betta not forgive shit
Don't let no preacher tell you I've gone on to a
better place
Matter of fact, let Mind Evolution eulogize me
Y'all better flip some tables
Snatch microphones
Occupy state houses
I love life and love
And my son
And poetry
I have purpose and vision and goals
I may be safe in the arms of the Savior
But
I don't believe this was the plan God had for me
when He knit me in my mother's womb
If they should come for me
Tell my son I had every intention of coming
home to him
And if love alone were powerful enough to keep
me here
I would never leave
Tell him I'm watching
Surround him
Let him be angry

Direct his anger and don't let him forget he is
brilliant
And if his father should shed a single tear
Slap his ass
Because I never got a chance to do it myself
Don't let them tell you I resisted arrest
If my claws have left tattoos on their faces and
necks
It is because I would not submit to death
I was not ready
Let this poem be a testimony
Every time I leave my house
I'm always planning to come home
to tuck in my son
and
go to sleep
and
wake up again in the morning

Throw Him Back Thursday

He is the type to discover
you are the answer to his mama's prayers
a full three years after you gave up wishing he
would love you back
He think he Easter
Raising up from your buried dream
trying to resurrect your hope
interrupting the momentum of your full
recovery
you moved on
that woke his ass up out a coma
you should bring your dating life over to the
hospital
your happiness might could change a flat line
to a steady heart rate
You are a miracle!
He didn't know flowers could be gifts three
years ago
Now this dude got bouquets on Thursdays
new love must be aromatic
he smelled you gazing into the eyes of another
or staring at your own reflection
in admiration and wonderment
or accidently stumbled into a memory of the
arch of your bronze back
or he missed your wanting
missed your needing

missed the way you used to work at being
deserving
your desperation was good for his posture
he finally figured out why his shoulders were
slumping
and came looking for a realignment
tell him to bring those calla lilies to the nearest
cemetery
decorate a grave
you are too alive to entertain a ghost

Risky Business

Mean mouth
sweet heart
safe heart
aloof
indifferent
safe heart
nothing lasts anymore
nobody is faithful
I am too much of this
Ain't got enough of that
Who is going to want-

Dear Heart,
You are the perfect fit for somebody
You are an answer to a prayer
You are not too old, too broke, or too broken to
be eligible
Everything you got and don't got is exactly
what somebody needs, been looking for
You are enough
You are the one and only for somebody
You and a special somebody might could win
this whole thing; together.
Love may be your color
have you ever asked yourself: what is the best
that could happen?
You can keep your heart safe
but your dreams are in danger

lay all your cards on the table
be the first to say the three words
believe everything she tells you
give him a secret to hold
let your guard go off duty for a little bit
it is better to have loved
get some guts
get a new ending to your story
your heart can handle it

Tender Love
A not so well kept secret:
The male psyche is
Delicate
An early bruise in their development
Can leave them forever tender
So we all tiptoe
around the landmines of the male ego
because ain't nothing more dangerous than a
man who feels the need to prove he ain't fragile
We
exit stage left
withdrawing from arguments
We know
the last bullet in the verbal chamber could
shatter a dream
When we are too complete
too tall
too influential
too self-sufficient
too experienced
too traveled
then they must be
less boss
have less control
they unravel
"who's the man?"
they need a distinction
we smile sweet

don't let the hair grow where it wants to
play damsel so they can play hero
silently laugh at the way the word pussy is used
to describe someone who lacks strength and
boldness
same word we use to describe the canal that
can accommodate a 10lb baby and clench a
climax out a linebacker
"The Weaker Sex"
We wear flat shoes
So they don't have to look up
hurts their neck and their pride
we don't want to hurt em
or confuse them into thinking they are our
opposition
we want to love em
we need them

Early

It is an act of resistance
Not calling
Not wondering who else he is calling because
he ain't calling you
Not telling everybody you are about to get all
the way in love, because you have been
mistaken about things like this before, even
though he is different and you are right this
time
not being concerned with his unusually fine
former significant other who seems to still be
his friend-she ain't finer than you
not hitting the snooze in the morning because
you told him you used to run and he thought
you meant recently and you didn't correct him
and you don't want him to think you a liar plus
you ate like an entire pan of cornbread
he didn't call her today
and he really wanted to call but he called her
twice yesterday and left a voicemail and
voicemail is evidence of sweat and he don't
sweat nobody but something funny happened
and he thought he could make her laugh and
her laugh is like jazz and her body is like reggae
sunsplash
she played his voicemail 18 times in a row and
panicked when she almost deleted it
then she deleted it because that was crazy

she wishes she saved it
he is potential
his middle name is Emmanuel and everybody
knows that is the name of her first son, if she
ever has a son
the night they met
that nosey broad from payroll gonna ask if he
was her brother, said he looked familiar,
probably why she kissed him, make the office
gossip more juicy
he kissed her a little bit, at the bar, people all
around, her eyes were closed
she didn't blame her inhibitions on the wine
he liked that
she is a surprise
she sent him a text that said "Home" like she
promised
he might be home too...

Taco Tuesday
A snapshot of three friends eating tacos a
pitcher of margaritas on the table
Heads tilted back in laughter good times a-
plenty
Pops up in your newsfeed
Your friends
You check your phone for missed messages
There are none
You like tacos
and margaritas
and laughing on a Tuesday
Imagine this moment was impromptu
Perhaps they all just happened to show up at
the same taco-margarita-laughing place at the
same time
You can't think of a good reason for them to
gather and deliberately exclude you- or worse,
not think of you at all
You made your own tacos anyway
and they are divine
You log off
Decide to make plans with a new friend, that
girl at work, what's her name?
Forget them!
and their dry jokes -
You get a text
"Throw on some clothes and meet us
downtown bitch!"

you're relieved
but you ain't going nowhere
You're bra is off, you are wearing sweats and
you don't feel like it
but
You love them hoes.

Shame the Devil

They are at your elbows
They are shifting the chanting of Whore and
Liar
to Goddess and Fearless
they are with you
Stilling the tremble in your voice
When you speak
You will set them free
he did not conquer you
You are as brilliant now
You are as vicious now
You are as woman now
as you were before he pushed his way inside
you
he did not know you were a warrior
they are waiting
bitten and swallowed tongues
buttoned lips
speak their hurt
truth his lies
they will find their mouths
brave yourself a posture
they will come behind you
catching arrows
they owe you their freedom
their silence armed your assailant
name him
they will echo

be the first to speak
and the last woman he ever attempts to destroy

Seasonal
Used to be
no such thing as hours
minutes and seconds was obsolete
my calendar
was drawn up in seasons
When he is here
When he was just here
When he ain't here
When he's bout to come back
The lonely fell on me heavy while he was gone
started to ask myself questions I couldn't
answer
"why would he want you?"
Truth be told
the season of Bout to Come Back
was my spring
the preparation for his return was full of ritual
cleaning
singing
fantasies of good lovin
fantasies of making him extend his leave of
absence from the place he called home
His arrival was never as fulfilling as I'd
imagined
we fought
our exchanges were more relief than pleasure
insults were his foreplay
we wore a hole in the novelty and by default

his welcome
he left
I burned some sage
bought myself a watch
edited my memories to replay in ways that
made me feel less
foolish
asked better questions
like
"Why would I want him?"
Couldn't answer that either

Self-Care

I got tired of feeling the way I was feeling
Had almost quit myself
So, I called myself
Invited myself
Welcomed myself
Gave myself an examination
Exposed all the buried parts of myself
Unsubscribed to all the lies I been telling
myself
Heard from God
Myself
Forgave myself
Painted my toes and washed my hair
Hugged myself
Laid myself down
Rocked myself to sleep
Dreamed a greater existence
Woke myself
Impregnated myself
Gave birth to myself
And child don't you know I spit myself out?
Nursed myself
Raised myself
Learned myself
Quieted myself
Amazed myself
Protected my Self
Laughed with myself

And gave myself permission to never ask
nobody permission
Allowed myself
Wrote myself
Sent love out into the atmosphere and caught it
when it came back myself
I do this every morning.

Shame off You

Your heart
twice healed already
still tender where it was punctured last
still pumping
still capable of opening
not short on memory
just ferociously brave
it knows its purpose
blessed thing
risking further injury
because
there are rewards
affection and kinship
a partner in crime in success and in worship
a shoulder built to catch your tears
a quick look that shares an inside joke and only
you know the punch line
someone who will be the face you look for after
you bury your parents
someone to remind you there is still someone
left on earth who prays for you after you've
buried your parents
someone your parents liked
someone you can hold up and help out
someone you can give all the things you have
been saving
you in all your vulnerable glory
are not a fool

to believe someone was who they said they
were
your offering was truth
they had no truth to give
you are not a fool
to not anticipate fraud
you are a soldier
and you didn't die
not even a little bit
Shout that from a mountaintop.
or keep it private
but shame is apt to ripen where there is too
much secret
leave some space between your chin and your
chest
you are no one's fool
anyone who tells you different
ain't got a heart as sturdy as yours
shame off you
go love some more

Global Mourning
The earth is shrouded in purple
Death caught us by surprise
Again
Snatched a star right out the sky
again
refused to let us pretend
it's safe to believe in life expectancy
these borrowed bodies
no matter how full of gift and sound and
miracle
get a little time to dance
before they are called away
but this one
even in eternal rest will continue to rock a
party
will still be responsible for babies being
conceived decades from today
strangers and enemies alike will touch and
agree on Adore as that jam
emerging musical artists of every genre will
attempt to purify themselves in the waters of
Lake Minnetonka to achieve even a morsel of
his influence
he left too much of himself behind
to ever really be missed
We still crying though
and wondering if we created anything that will
continue to breathe when we can't anymore

Proper Love

I am the absolute best version of myself when I
am being loved properly.
You should see me when I am getting as many
kisses on my neck as I want
I use fewer words when there is someone who
understands my non-talk
I am regal as fuck
When oil is being massaged into my scalp on
the regular
Peep the shine I put on the floor when I am
made to be a priority
Have you ever tasted an omelet prepared by a
woman who prayed you would finally show up?
Spend a weekend with me
Come Monday you will be hating on your
Saturday night self
Just tell me no one can do for you what I can
do for you anytime you get the inclination
My credit score will climb 200 points
Include me in your plans
And I'll awaken every morning without the aid
of an alarm with the solution to somebody's
problem
Say things to me like "Your car was making a
funny noise, but don't worry about baby! I
took care of it."
You don't even have to buy me nothing.
Just appreciate my style.

Ask me when I am going to wear that dress
again with those shoes so you can show me off.
I will strut everywhere.
While simultaneously reciting Einstein's theory
of relativity.
In Mandarin
You can almost hear my I.Q. expanding
From all that good loving
Baby
You, holding back on your adoration of me is a
little bit illegal
Might be detrimental to the planet
Love me ferocious so I can be great.
Fuck around and find a Pulitzer hanging out
my back pocket
Love my son
Treat him like you are the one who put him in
my belly
Assemble his bike while I nap on the couch
Teach him some man shit
I promise you'll think it's your birthday when I
get through with you
Forgive me for needing so much, Partner
As extraordinary as I am now
There is greatness I cannot reach
Just imagine the fire I could unleash
The world needs you to ignite me
Bring your whole self here right now
And love me properly.

Made in the USA
Columbia, SC
16 February 2018